CATS

CATS

Tom Howard

WHSMITH
EXCLUSIVE
·BOOKS·

This edition produced exclusively for W H Smith

Published by
Octopus International
a division of Reed International Books Limited,
Michelin House, 81 Fulham Road, London SW3 6RB

ISBN 0 600 57413 X

Printed in Hong Kong

CONTENTS

INTRODUCTION

What is it that makes a cat such a delight to have around? For some people it is the cat's physical grace and beauty, or its obvious intelligence, for others it is its cosy comforting companionship. Psychologists tell us that just stroking a cat's fur can create a sense of calm and relaxation. Cats have great personality and maintain a definite independence. Though often showing a great desire to be involved with people and lavish in their displays of affection, they will disappear about their own business to pursue a lifestyle quite separate from any domestic conditioning.

All these things contribute to the cat's appeal and the cat is rapidly becoming the most popular of household pets. Yet, of all the animals which man has domesticated it is probably the least changed from its natural state. It is only in comparatively recent times that breeders have intervened to produce new breeds and types – a process which has been going on for thousands of years with dogs, horses and other domestic animals. It is not for nothing that the cat has been called 'the tiger on the hearth'.

It is difficult to observe the lives of most mammals, especially the nocturnal hunters, but the cat offers an opportunity for everyone to study the complete life cycle and behaviour of an animal at close quarters in their own homes and backyards. This book draws attention to many aspects of feline life, explaining the behaviour patterns which you can see for yourself if you take the trouble to observe the cats around you.

THE CAT WITH NINE LIVES

Who would think that a cat sitting calmly in the sun or fastidiously washing a paw could live a life of risk and danger? Yet cats have earned a proverbial nine lives from their ability to survive. This is not due to any mystical protection but to a very efficient physique and well-developed senses, although cats can still make mistakes and they have their share of disasters. In some respects their skills outshine those of their owners but there are other areas where their abilities are not so good.

Cats have a very flexible skeleton and good musculature. They can turn their heads, for instance, almost 180° each way, much more than humans. They can produce great spurts of power but because their heart and lungs are comparatively small (more body space is taken up by their digestive system), they cannot sustain activity for long.

Jumping up on to a wall five times its own height or leaping across a stream offers no problem to the average cat; its powerful hind legs provide tremendous thrust. Jumping downwards it will reduce the height by first stretching down, then trying to push outwards. This gives it more chance of lowering its hind feet during the drop in order to make a four-point landing, and so lessen the impact to be absorbed by each paw.

If they fall from a height, cats are able to turn in the air to align themselves for landing but too forceful an impact can still cause injury, often a fractured palate. Cats falling from heights which enable them to reach maximum velocity before landing are less likely to be injured for, once the speed of fall is steady, they relax, which makes for a softer touchdown.

A cat's claws can be vicious weapons but when they are sheathed a cat has a velvet touch and a near silent tread. Each sharp curved claw helps the cat gain purchase, even on apparently smooth surfaces, and they are ideal for climbing trees. Cats like climbing and they also enjoy looking down on things.

Getting back to earth again is not so easy. As a cat climbs a tree it stretches out a paw, grips and pulls itself up, hanging from its claws. However, the claws curve the wrong way for supporting a head-first vertical descent. Walking down a slope is no problem but an upright tree trunk requires a backwards action, the cat lowering itself until it is near enough to ground level to twist around and jump safely.

Cats have an excellent sense of balance; this involves structures within the inner ear known as the 'vestibular apparatus', which used to be thought somehow different from ours – but tightrope walkers develop similar skills. Although cats use their tails in balance control, Manx and other tailless cats do not seem to be handicapped.

Cats have good spatial sense, squeezing through small holes and rarely bumping into things. It is often thought that their whiskers grow to the width of their bodies and act as a measure of whether they can get through spaces. Whiskers certainly play a part for, together with similar hairs on the backs of the front paws, they are sensitive to air pressure which subtly changes according to the position of surrounding objects.

Watch a cat's ears prick up when it hears something of interest; they are extremely flexible and can turn a full half circle in the direction of the sound. Cats' sharp hearing is not so effective as our own in the lower ranges but extends much higher, well into the range of bats' sonic squeaks. Cats learn to ignore all kinds of general noises but react instantly to any sounds which have a relevance to their lives. Out of the general murmur of traffic they will recognize the family car's engine or identify the footsteps of a friend long before they reach the house. Being able to hear and locate the slightest rustle in the undergrowth or barnyard straw is a great asset to the hunter.

Smell is of immense importance to a cat. It carries vital information about food, about dangers, about sex and about territory. This ginger and white cat smelling a twig has registered that it has been sprayed by a dog and has slightly raised its tail fur, a reaction to a potential threat.

The membrane sensitive to smell in the cat's nose covers nearly twice the area it does in humans, and cats also have an additional scent organ between nose and palate, known as Jacobson's organ. You will often see a cat sitting with its mouth slightly open in an expression of apparent disdain – known by scientists as the 'flehmen' reaction. The cat is actually sucking in scent particles and transferring them from its tongue to channels behind the upper teeth which connect with this scent organ.

Cats can't really see in the dark, they must rely upon their other senses, but their eyes are adapted to make full use of any available light however dim. In bright light the pupils of their eyes narrow to a tiny slit, preventing dazzle; as it gets dark they open wide to admit as much as possible. A surface at the back of the eye then reflects light forward, enabling it to use that light twice over. It is this that makes a cat's eyes appear to shine in the dark.

Humans have a sharper focus and much better colour vision than the cat but these are not much use in dim light and the cat's eyes are much better adapted to the world of the night hunter.

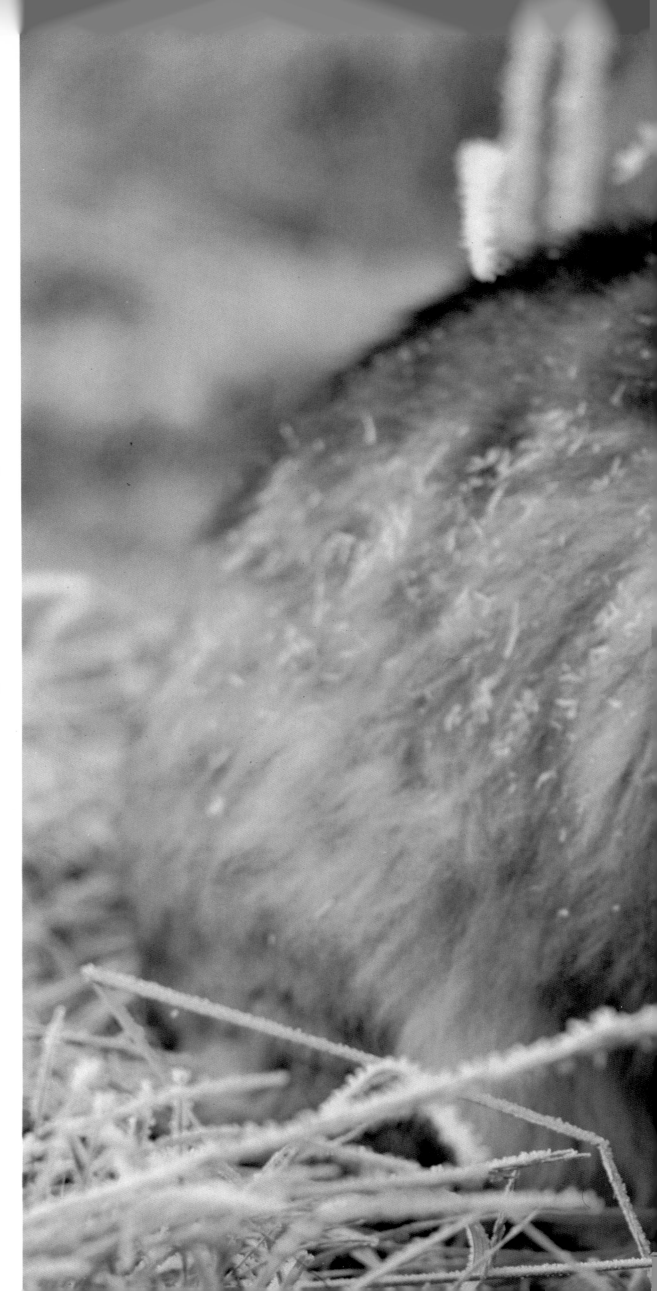

Like all mammals, cats are warm blooded. Except when tiny kittens, or under very extreme conditions, they are able to maintain their body temperature at an even level and be active at all times, unlike reptiles which must wait for the sun to warm them up. Their furry coat provides insulation against heat loss.

The types of cat which were first domesticated had short fur, and longhaired cats, especially those which have been selectively bred to have very luxuriant coats, are not always able to take care of them on their own. Show cats need a lot of grooming and even domestic pets should have a daily brushing.

When parents are of a different coat type or colour short fur is always dominant over long, and tabby over single colours and other patterns. Red colour is caused by a gene carried on the pair of chromosomes which determine sex and though a male can inherit the red colouring it is theoretically not possible for it to inherit the combination of genes to produce a tortoiseshell coat of red, black and cream; although the occasional male tortoiseshell appears, due to a rare chromosome imbalance, such cats are nearly always sterile.

From parents' pedigrees breeders can predict the colour and body type of kittens. Once a particular type exists carefully selected matings can produce a whole range of colours.

The Chinchilla (right) is one of the most beautiful of cats. Its long, silky white fur is tipped with black, giving the coat a sparkling appearance. The brick red nose and the blue-green or emerald eyes are outlined in black adding to its dazzling appearance.

Eye colour is inherited independently of coat colour but blue eyes when linked with white fur are associated with deafness in cats. Kittens born with even the smallest area of coloured fur, even though it disappears when they mature, are not genetically white, and so are unaffected, but odd-eyed white cats, as above, are sometimes deaf in just one ear.

When people first began to exhibit cats competitively it was the long-haired Persian cats which attracted most attention with their luxuriant fur. Pale coats with colour restricted to the face, tail and limbs – a 'pointed' pattern like that of the Siamese, were a much later development and some people classify them as a different breed, the Colourpoints (left and above). Long furred or short, sleek and elegant or short and stocky, blue-blooded pedigree or alley cat, each animal has its own individual character. Personality can vary more between cat and cat than can be categorized as particular to a breed. Yet, different though each may be, all share those instincts, skills and behaviour patterns which mark them out as distinctively cats.

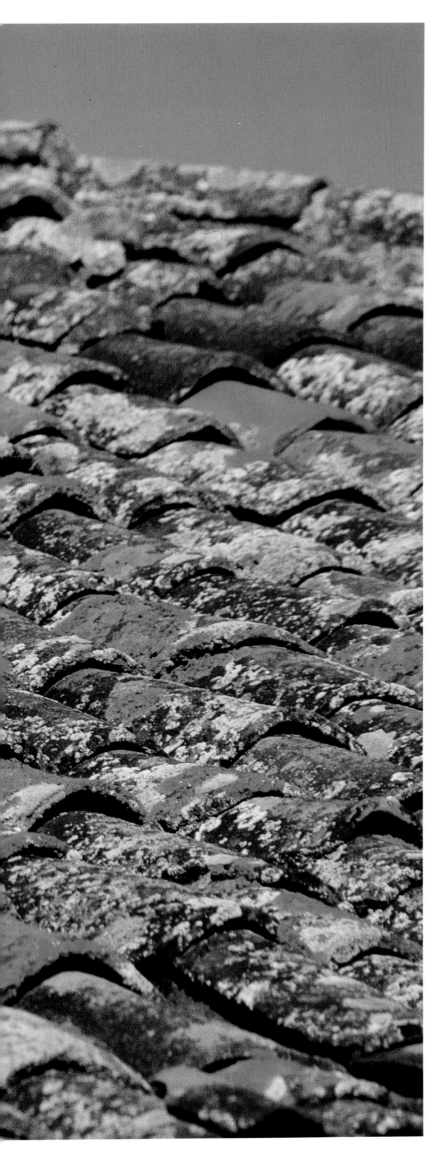

CAT BEHAVIOUR

The cat has evolved as an efficient predator but however perfect its hunter's physique it will starve if it has no prey to catch. It must establish a hunting territory and, within that, a core territory which is likely to be rigorously defended. Territory size will reflect both prey supply and the pressure of feline numbers. Even domestic cats, which have no need to hunt for food, have a strong sense of territory.

A newcomer has to find its own patch, perhaps driving out a cat already claiming its back yard. Territorial boundaries can be very complex. A cat may not have claim to the roof it lives beneath and a garden may be divided between several cats, none of whom live in the house to which it belongs.

A cat marks its territory at various points, not necessarily its perimeter, by spraying urine, by scratching, which leaves a scent mark from the paw pads as well as the visible signs, and by rubbing its body against objects, bringing scent secreting glands on the temples, chin and base of the tail into contact.

Marking is not necessarily a signal to keep out, more of a calling card. Cats will investigate a point marked by another cat with interest not fear. Although territory will be defended against a cat who tries to take it over there is rarely any attempt to prevent another passing through and often, especially in urban areas, there will be areas which are shared.

P et cats that have no choice but to share a home, and siblings that stay together into maturity will often share a core territory, but each may have a wider range of its own and special places within the core to which it lays claim. They may be prepared to allow another cat to join them in their personal space, provided that their prior claim is acknowledged. Sometimes, although not always, an hierarchy develops in cat colonies. Often it is not the toughest customer in the group but an old cat, mother and grandmother of the rest, to whom the others defer.

Group living can have advantages: mutual grooming, the warmth of company on cold nights and the help of 'aunties' to look after young kittens.

Cats have a wide range of vocal signals from the soft chirrups with which a mother cat communicates with her kittens to the strident call of the female ready to mate, and from the crooning courtship murmurs of the male to sleep-shattering caterwauling. Cats, like us, have individual voices, usually recognized by the way in which they pronounce vowel sounds. Owners soon learn to recognize demands for attention, for food, for litter trays to be changed or for a door to be opened – even a rather curt sounding mew that means 'thank you' – and everyone knows the purr of a contented cat. What no one knows for sure is exactly how the purring sound is made.

The cat's body language is often easier for people to interpret than their meows. Position of ears, tail, body and fur, facial expression and general demeanour can all be very indicative of mood and of intention. Most obvious is the confident tail held high, the tip often curling forward, which signals greeting. An upright tail, bristling like a bottle brush, should be read as a slight threat, an arched back as a defensive threat. A tail lashing from side to side warns that a cat is really annoyed and close to doing something about it.

When cat friends meet they rub against each other, often touching noses, then move their faces against the other's body, caressing them with their tails, each leaving their scent on the other. With humans they often curl around our legs.

Cats have ways of reaching awkward places to keep them clean but it is easier when they wash them for each other; a helping tongue is rarely turned away. Mutual grooming is a frequent activity between siblings and friendly cats. Grooming is often offered to dominant cats by other cats who want to appease them.

Most cats enjoy a regular grooming from their owner, purring contentedly as a human friend does all the work. They should be familiarized with a brush and comb when they are kittens. They obviously delight in the physical sensation but part of the pleasure probably comes from being given so much attention.

Cats usually avoid confrontation and only fight as a last resort. They go through a series of preliminary manoeuvres to try to resolve the situation without actually coming to blows. After an exchange of threats and posturings one will usually acknowledge the other's superiority, indicating submission by making itself seem as small as possible, often crouching low with ears flattened forwards.

The familiar arched back and fluffed-up fur is created by a combination of reactions as fear encourages the cat to retreat and bravado tells it to advance. Almost all confrontations show a mixture of threatening and defensive response.

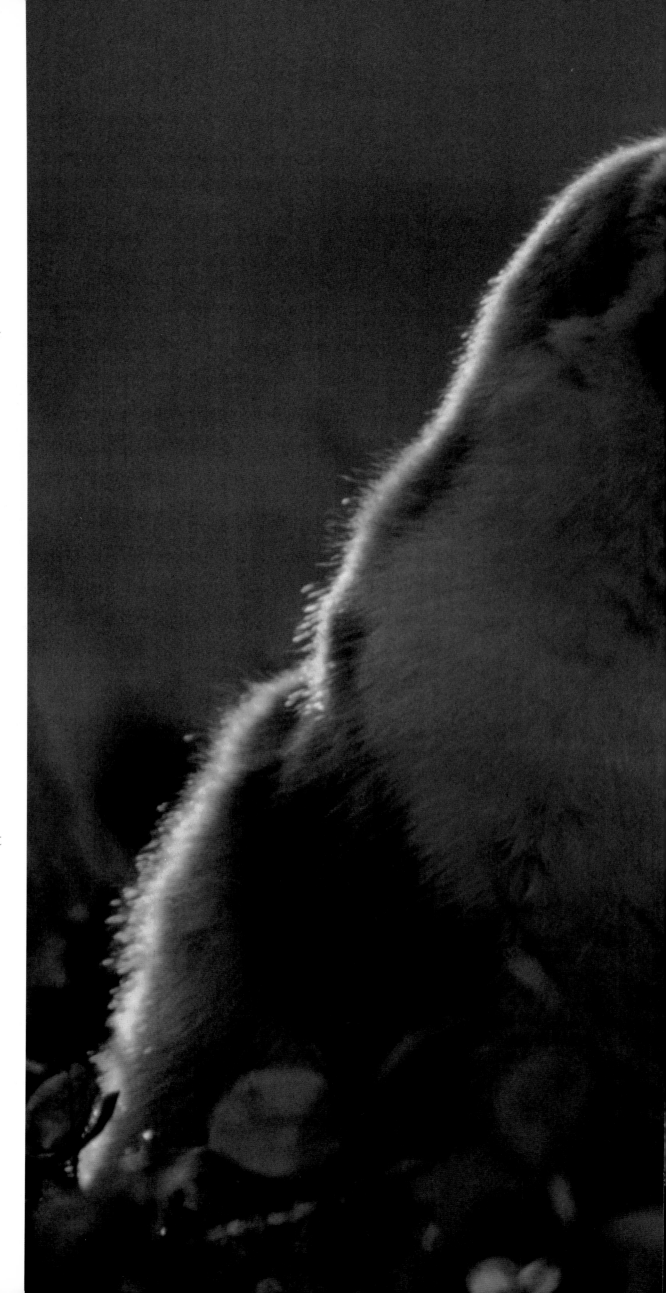

Cats evolved as nocturnal hunters, being most efficient in the half light of dusk and early morning. The domestic pet retains its hunting instincts and will chase and catch, but unless introduced to live prey by its mother, a kitten will not necessarily connect hunting for prey with food.

Cats have two main hunting techniques: stalking and ambush. A cat will wait patiently next to a mouse hole or beside a route along which prey is known to pass, ready to pounce when a suitable victim appears. Experienced cats will not spring on a mouse the moment it emerges from a hole – it might be able to bolt back inside again. They wait until it has come too far to dive back to safety.

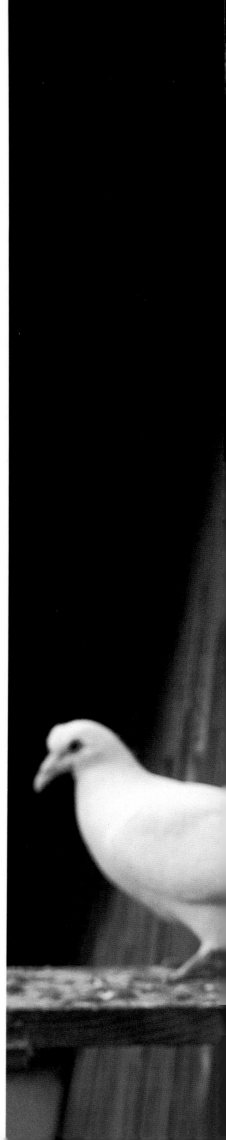

S een almost in monochrome by prey animals, most cats are very well camouflaged among grasses and undergrowth but they make themselves even less noticeable by keeping their bodies close to the ground. Moving quickly through thick cover or crossing open ground they approach very stealthily when they think prey are near, getting as close as possible before making the final attack and freezing mid-movement if there is any risk they have been spotted.

A cat watching a bird that is out of reach or through a window often makes a chattering, staccato sound. Why, is a mystery. Is it excitement or a sign of irritation, a challenge or a threat?

Sleep accounts for up to two-thirds of a cat's
life. Wild cats are active at night but domestic
pets, especially if allowed to sleep on their
owner's bed, often adapt themselves to human life
patterns. They may not sleep the whole night in a
single stretch and will still often sleep during the
day, especially if their people are out. The normal
sleep pattern consists of many shortish periods.
Much of the time this is shallow sleep, when the cat
can register external stimuli and respond to
danger. For periods of six or seven minutes this
can become deep sleep when the cat is completely
relaxed. It is then a cat may dream – but the
twitching of paws and whiskers does not mean it is
pursuing a dream hunt. It is merely a discharge of
surplus electrical energy in the muscles.

THE CAT'S DAY

Adult cats do not waste energy. In the wild, strenuous effort is reserved for hunting and other necessary activity. Cats will have a main sleeping place at the heart of their core territory – curled up on their owner's bed for many domestic pets – but will catnap in all kinds of unlikely places, often having a succession of spots to fit different conditions or times of day.

They like fixed hours for meals, play sessions, grooming and being let out to socialize and hunt (and being let in again), all matched to a regular routine. They have a good sense of time and will probably let you know if you do not keep to the schedule.

The first activity on waking is usually a good stretch followed by a wash – unless it has been a long sleep and a toilet call is needed. 'If in doubt, wash' seems to be the cats' catechism. Cats are always washing – partly because they like to be clean, partly as a displacement activity to hide embarrassment, give them time to think, distract attention from their real intentions, or pretend that they are just not interested. A cat's tongue is covered with backward pointing sharp papillae which form a rasp, ideal for scraping flesh off bones and an efficient washcloth and hairbrush. Where the tongue cannot reach cats clean with a tongue-moistened paw. Washing is also a way to keep cool in hot weather, evaporation of saliva from the fur helps to reduce their temperature.

Cats find it very satisfying to dig their claws into a piece of wood or furniture and have a good stretch. This is quite different from deliberate scratching, which is used as a marker. Another form of scratching 'sharpens' the claws – not really sharpening but removing the blunted outer layer to reveal a sharp new tip. Cats usually have a favourite place for this activity – which may also be scratch marked. If it is a piece of furniture it can be very badly damaged. Luckily cats are easily trained to use a log or a piece of coarse cloth mounted on a stand or against the wall. Notice whether your cat prefers to perform this action on the floor or against a vertical before deciding what to offer for its use.

C ats have always got an eye and ear open for a friend, even a stranger well-disposed to cats, who can be cajoled into giving them some attention. A roll upon the ground with the belly exposed is a bold declaration that a cat wants to be friends and an invitation to play or pet.

Some cats like to have their exposed tummy tickled but beware, not all find this acceptable and the presentation of the underparts, which to another cat is a clear indication of submission by offering the most vulnerable body area, also brings into play a pair of powerful weapons – the hind legs and their claws. A cat that does not like being tickled may defend itself by giving you a raking slash.

All kittens play games, it is part of the learning process. Since one of the effects of domestication is to preserve some infantile characteristics, including play, the adult pet has a much stronger tendency to play than do wild feline species. Play behaviour will be especially strong where it is maintained by regular games with human companions. It may range from chasing string to football, retrieving and hide-and-seek. A game with a partner, animal or human, is usually preferred, but lots of cats will also play on their own.

B ack home again, a good scratch to get the circulation going and dislodge any bits picked up on the fur, is followed by another wash. Then cats will usually circle a few times on the spot, an instinctive move to settle a nest out in the wild, and time for another nap – in front of a nice warm fire if possible. Cats really enjoy lying in the sun, on top of a boiler or near a radiator or an open fire. They often get so close that they singe their fur and can even have their tail right in a flame before they register the heat.

When confident and warm a cat will stretch its body wide, both to enjoy the heat and because there is no need to conserve it. In cold conditions a cat will curl up and surround itself with an insulating ball of fur, its tail tip probably covering its nose.

FAMILY LIFE

Cats usually make excellent mothers and most give birth with no problems whatsoever, although they have their share of breech births, stillbirths and Caesarians. The problem is not having kittens but how to find them homes. Although cats are now such popular pets there are still a great many unwanted kittens born and animal welfare organizations have to destroy thousands and thousands of cats and kittens every year. For the owner who is confident that homes are waiting for his or her cat's kittens there is nothing more delightful than seeing and sharing in the raising of a litter but otherwise spaying of females and neutering of all pet toms is the only way of ensuring that unwanted kittens are not born.

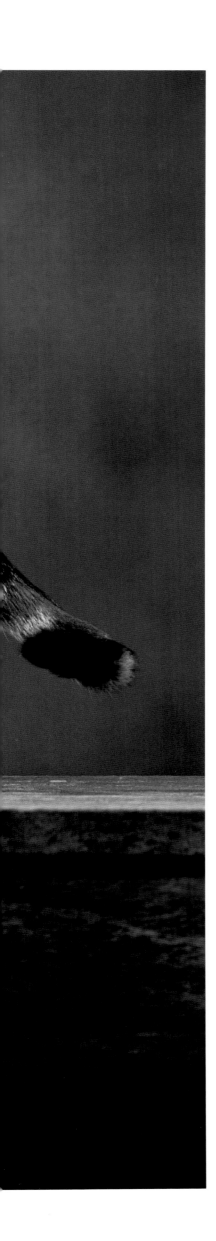

Pregnancy in the domestic cat lasts about nine weeks. There is little sign of it at first – just a pinking of the nipples – but the mother-to-be develops a bigger appetite. Life goes on as normal. Only at the fifth or sixth week is there any noticeable swelling. After seven weeks the mother will begin to seek out a suitable nest and a kittening box should be prepared for her. When it comes to giving birth instinct takes over. She will lick free the kitten from the membrane in which it is born, sever its umbilical cord and start it on its life. Cats that are very attached to their owners sometimes manage to delay birth until they have them by their side but help is rarely needed. Guided by smell the newborn kitten finds a nipple and is soon suckling happily.

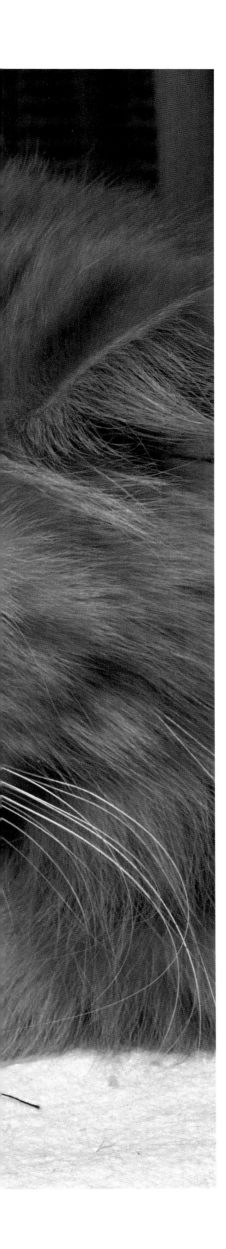

Kittens' eyes do not usually open until they are between five to ten days old and do not function properly for another week. It will be more than two months before they can see as well as adult cats. Blue at first, they change to their inherited shade at about three months old. The ears are folded down at birth and may take a fortnight or more to become erect, by which time they are oriented to natural sounds, although hearing is still far from adult sensitivity. The sense of smell nears mature levels by three weeks old. In their first three weeks kittens cannot regulate their body temperature and it takes another month before they control this fully. When mother has to leave them the litter clumps together to maintain body heat as much as possible.

Rearing kittens is a full-time job for mother. At first she will wake them and encourage them to suckle by curling her body around them – later they will demand feeding individually and at all hours. More than half her time may be taken up with suckling. Licking not only keeps them clean but stimulates digestion and defecation. When kittens are very young she can leave them only for a moment or they could die of cold but soon she has to go off to find food. As they begin to crawl about she will call them back if they stray too far or carry them to the nest by gripping the scruff of the neck between her teeth. Sometimes, if disturbed, she may even transport the whole litter to a new nest.

At about sixteen days old a kitten begins to crawl and by twice that age it will be able to move quite well, play with its brothers and sisters and begin to groom itself. At first kitten play is an interaction with littermates, experimenting with actions and responses that are used in the social life of cats: there are confrontations, even fights, and you will often see a kitten's fur standing on end as it tries to pretend that it is twice its size. Play is full of reversals. One kitten will chase another, leap upon it, then suddenly stop and run off, wanting to be chased itself.

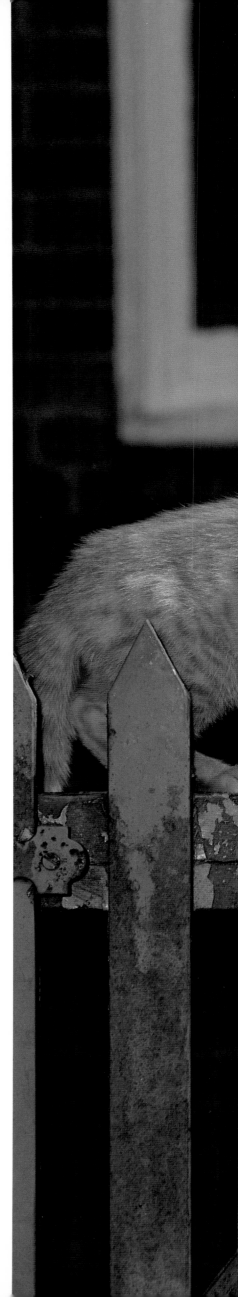

rowing kittens have to learn to use their bodies and to develop all those physical skills which they need to live the life of a cat to the full. They must learn to estimate the distance for a jump, to judge the energy that is needed to perform an action, to test out their balancing and acrobatic abilities, to climb (and to come down again). As their senses come into full operation they must learn to use them efficiently, to develop coordination and use effort to the best advantage. Everything is new and they make many mistakes but mother keeps a watchful eye on them. There are few real disasters and all the little ones probably help the learning process and can be put down to experience.

As kittens get older their sudden chases and rough-and-tumbles give place to different kinds of games. Pursuit is now much more controlled. As well as ambushes there will be stealthy creeping along the ground or behind cover. They begin to pounce on things with real purpose. They exercise much more paw control, hitting an object from paw to paw along the ground. They pick things up in their jaws and they use their small sharp teeth to bite. They are bringing into operation the techniques and skills they will use when hunting and dispatching prey. They learn to use their ears to identify the exact position of a rustling sound, to locate the object with their eyes and to advance with caution before a final spring.

For the young kitten everything in the world is new and has to be checked out. 'Hmm, that smell is interesting. What's that? Is there anything in there? What happens if . . . no perhaps its safer not to touch it. Oh! It moved! Jumped right over my head. Ah, that's a bird. I wonder – too late it flew away. Gotcha! well, flies taste good. Sniff, that dog's been here, not long ago. Careful, he may be just around the corner. Safer to go home. Well, there's no one in the kitchen or the hall, let's try in here. That looks worth investigating, might be a useful place to hide. Ah, smells of lavender and the legs that give mother her food and the hands that pick me up . . . What? Oh its mother calling. Better go or I'll be in trouble . . . Ooops, I don't remember climbing up that far! . . .'

E xploring the world is not all plain sailing.
Things are not always as easy as they look.
Having discovered how easy it is to climb up a
tree a kitten then has to face the problem of getting
down again and discovers that that requires a
different technique. Many things a kitten must learn
for itself, and the process will go on long after
it has grown up.

Dealing with other animals is another area in
which a kitten gains experience. Fortunately many
animals show a general tolerance of the young even
of other species and though a kitten may go through
the whole range of confrontational postures they will
not be provoked. If the kitten is not so lucky its
tree-climbing technique could come in useful.

At eight weeks old a kitten should have a full set of teeth teeth and be fully weaned on to solid food, although that does not mean that it will not attempt to suckle if it sees the opportunity. By this time, many cat mothers probably find the kittens' teeth are making their nipples sore and are becoming irritated by constant demands for milk, even though they are still producing it. The kittens have now developed considerable independence, although there are still many things they can learn from their mother and from interaction with brothers and sisters. Domestic pets should not leave for their new homes until they are twelve weeks old; in the wild the family would stay together much longer before going off to establish their own territories.

Everyone is charmed by a young kitten but deciding to have one as a pet should not be undertaken lightly. It means being responsible for another life for a long time to come, probably for fifteen or even twenty years – while the record for cat longevity is thirty-six! That can add up to a considerable outlay in money, time and effort, providing food, care and veterinary attention, planning your own life so that the cat is regularly fed and making arrangements for it to be looked after if you are away on holiday or business. But the pleasure a cat can give will make it all worthwhile and, as Mark Twain wrote: 'a home without a cat, and a well-fed, well-petted and properly revered cat, may be a perfect home, *perhaps*, but how can it prove its title?'

OUT IN THE WORLD

Leaving mother and siblings and settling into a new home is a traumatic experience for a kitten. Fortunately the excitement of exploring a new world takes up a lot of their time and attention. Meeting feline and other members of the new household can be intimidating – though a kitten is more easily accepted than an older animal which offers a greater territorial challenge.

Popular though cats are as pets, not every kitten finds a welcoming new home. Some who do, the centre of attention when they are very little, are neglected once their novelty wears off or even abandoned completely. They must take their chances with the many other feral cats that lead an independent life.

Farm cats are often halfway between domestic pets and feral animals. Though outsiders may occasionally be allowed to join the group they will usually have a basic core made up of several generations of one family. They will probably all hunt vermin within the core territory around the farm buildings, but each will have an individual range on the perimeter. When the population gets too large, weaker individuals will be forced further afield to find a personal territory and will have to relinquish any rights in the central territory.

Feeding and attention from the farmer will ensure that they stay on the farm. Keeping cats hungry does not make them keener hunters. Cats hunt because it is built into their behaviour and a strong and healthy cat is the more efficient hunter.

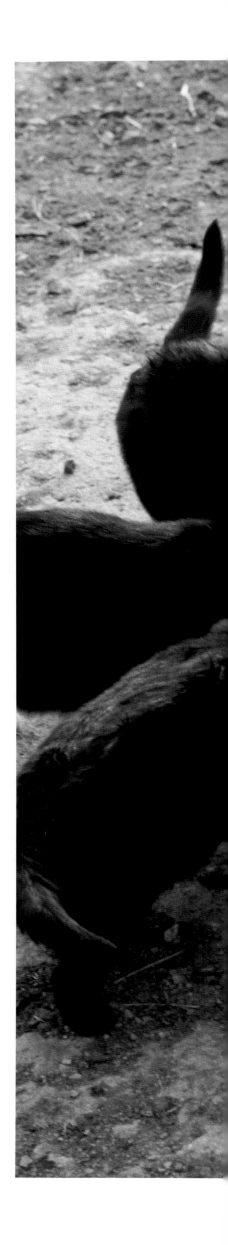

Feral cats become efficient scavengers, adept at spotting spilled milk and begging at tourist pavement restaurants as well as raiding garbage cans but *every* cat is an opportunist. Even the best-cared-for pet seems convinced that someone else's dinner must taste better than its own and that stolen food has a much better flavour. To leave food out unattended is asking for trouble even though a cat may seem a perfect angel when you are watching it. Puss knows that by the time he's climbed up to the bird table the prey will all have flown but it is their food, and not the birds, he's after.

As naturalist Gilbert White observed, it is strange that cats, which usually have a distaste for getting wet, so enjoy a fishy diet. They will often watch fish swimming in a pond or stream for hours and some manage to become adept at putting in a paw and flipping them out. There are even authenticated cases – though only one or two – of cats which habitually dived in and brought fish out.

A cat which accidentally finds itself in the water will usually instinctively swim with a dog-paddle fore-paw action but they do not have the stamina to keep going for long.

Lucky the quayside cat who gets fresh fish each morning. It *may* be patient – it will get its own share soon – but cats find it very difficult to resist temptation!

ACKNOWLEDGEMENTS

Animal Photography/Sally Anne Thompson 20, 24, 80-1, 90-1; Animals Unlimited 1, 32, 72-3; Ardea 78, 80; Bruce Coleman/Jim Bain 43; Bruce Coleman/Jane Burton 2, 18-19, 27, 41, 53, 54-55, 58, 59, 66-7, 67, 69, 74-5, 82-3, 84, 85; Bruce Coleman/Jane Burton and Kim Taylor 10-11, 20-1; Bruce Coleman/Eric Crichton 5; Bruce Coleman/Hans Reinhard 6, 16, 22-3, 34-5, 37, 39, 46-7, 60-1, 68-9; Sally and Richard Greenhill 48, 93; Natural History Photographic Agency/Henry Ausloos 64-5; Stephen Dalton 76, 77; Octopus Publishing Group Ltd/Peter Loughran 29/John Moss 28, 32-3; Solitaire Photographic 26, 88, 88-9; Spectrum Colour Library 8-9, 12, 13, 14-15, 30-1, 42-3, 46, 49, 50-1, 56-7, 57, 62-3, 73, 92, 94-5; Zefa Picture Library 10, 17, 25, 36, 38, 40, 44-5, 52, 70-1, 74, 79, 86-7.